IMAGES
of America

VANISHED
SAN FRANCISCO

The huge Mark Hopkins mansion was built on California Street atop Nob Hill. The building on the far left was Leland Stanford's home. It was large but obviously much smaller than Hopkins's. His building was later donated to San Francisco for the Mark Hopkins Institute of Art. It burned down in the fire after the 1906 earthquake. (Courtesy of the San Francisco History Center, San Francisco Public Library.)

ON THE COVER: The Crystal Palace Market was an unusual shopping experience. The 70,000-square-foot market operated at Eighth and Market Streets from 1923 to 1959. Customers could buy food products, but vendors also sold unusual foods, special services, and large appliances. Originally built on what was considered the outskirts of San Francisco, the market encouraged the spread of business and development down Market Street. (Courtesy of the San Francisco Department of Public Works.)

IMAGES
of America

VANISHED
SAN FRANCISCO

Lorri Ungaretti

ARCADIA
PUBLISHING

Published by Arcadia Publishing
Charleston, South Carolina

Printed in the United States of America

Library of Congress Control Number: 2022944860

For all general information, please contact Arcadia Publishing:
Telephone 843-853-2070
Fax 843-853-0044
E-mail sales@arcadiapublishing.com
For customer service and orders:
Toll-Free 1-888-313-2665

Visit us on the Internet at www.arcadiapublishing.com

CONTENTS

ACKNOWLEDGMENTS

I feel the greatest appreciation to John Freeman, a local historian, writer, and lecturer—and a good enough friend that he was willing to review the information in this book.

I am indebted to the following people who shared photographs and information with me: Marilyn Blaisdell, Richard Brandi, Robert Bryant, Chris Carlsson, Patricia Carpenter, Lana Costantini, Rita Dunn, Emiliano Echeverria, LisaRuth Elliot, Bruce Eng, Edie Epps, John Freeman, Greg Gaar, Thomas Gille, Gary Goss, Bennett Hall, Ron Henggeler, Gary Kurutz, Richard Lim, Peter Linenthal, Angus Macfarlane, Nicole Meldahl, Phil Milholton, Dennis Minnick, Dennis O'Rorke, John Rampley, Evelyn Rose, Susan Saperstein, Anne Schnoebelen, James Smith, Alex Spotorno, Alan Thomas, Jack Tillmany, Paul Totah, Harold Tuchfeld, Arnold Woods, and a few anonymous private collectors.

As usual, I give a special thanks for the great ideas, insights, and guidance of Christina Moretta and the other librarians in the San Francisco History Center at the San Francisco Public Library.

I also appreciate the generosity of the following organizations for providing photographs and guidance for this book:

Archdiocese of San Francisco
Bancroft Library
Glen Park Neighborhoods History Project
Library of Congress
National Park Service
OpenSFHistory
Pacific Gas & Electric Co.
San Francisco Archives
San Francisco Chronicle
San Francisco Department of Public Works
San Francisco Historical Society
San Francisco History Center, San Francisco Public Library
San Francisco Zoo
San Jose State University Special Collection and Archives
Sutro Library Branch, California State Library
University of California, San Francisco
The U.S. National Archives and Records Administration (National Archives)
Western Neighborhoods Project
Xerces Society for Invertebrate Conservation (Xerces.org)

INTRODUCTION

The houses, businesses, and other features of San Francisco in this book existed at one time in the city and for various reasons have disappeared. Items that have been remodeled or reused—for example, Ghirardelli Square in San Francisco, which once contained businesses (a chocolate factory, a woolen mill, and more) and is now used for shops, restaurants, and condominiums—are not included. The book just includes things that no longer exist.

Many reasons exist for the disappearance of things in San Francisco, but many of these changes can be traced to one of four reasons: natural causes, such as an earthquake; major fires; human desire to replace items with something "better"; or changes in people's interests or behavior.

San Francisco is a relatively young city, yet it has experienced more change than many cities around the United States. As a result, unlike other parts of the country that have buildings dating back to the 1700s, San Francisco does not have any buildings older than the 1800s (except for Mission Dolores). San Francisco does have many Victorian buildings, which residents consider old, but they only date back about 120 to 150 years. This concentration of younger buildings is not just in San Francisco or California; the oldest buildings in the western half of the United States (except in Texas) tend to be from the mid-1800s.

The quiet town of Yerba Buena, which became San Francisco in 1847, was forever changed by the California Gold Rush starting in January 1848. Once word spread that gold had been discovered close to the town of Coloma (about 130 miles northeast of San Francisco), people came from around the world. The population of the area exploded. The quiet hamlet of San Francisco had fewer than 500 residents in 1847. By late 1849, about 1,000 people were arriving every week. By December 1850, the population of San Francisco was 25,000. By 1856, it was 56,000.

San Francisco residents in the early 1850s lived in quick-to-construct canvas tents and ramshackle wooden sheds. It was important to build simply and quickly, then travel to the gold country to make one's fortune. But these poorly built residences were vulnerable to fire.

At least six destructive fires burned in San Francisco between December 1849 and June 1851. After each fire, people built quickly, usually with the same flammable materials. Each subsequent fire seemed to destroy more buildings than the one before.

Portsmouth Square (then called the Plaza)—bounded by Kearny, Washington, and Grant Streets and Walter U. Lum Place—was a central meeting place in the city, with hotels, courts of law, stores, offices, and the custom house. A lot of people conducted business and socialized in Portsmouth Square, and when fire erupted in the area, many significant buildings burned.

The major fires broke out on December 24, 1849; May 4, 1850; June 14, 1850; September 17, 1850; May 4, 1851 (by far the most destructive); and June 22, 1851.

More than 100 years later, in December 1940, the official City and County of San Francisco flag was adopted; it features a phoenix rising above flames, a clear nod to the city's history.

The upper part of the *Niantic*, one of the many ships abandoned in San Francisco Bay, was burned in the second great San Francisco fire in May 1851. A hotel that was built on the hull was destroyed in the fire in 1906. Other buildings in this book destroyed by fire include the Cliff House (1907), Baldwin Hotel and Theatre, St. Paulus Church, the second St. Mary's Cathedral, Beach Chalet, Ewing Field, and Tait's at the Beach.

Earthquakes occurred frequently in San Francisco in the 1800s, including in 1812, 1827, 1850, 1865, and other years. But nothing was like the earthquake of 1906, which became known around the world. The Richter scale had not yet been invented, but the magnitude of the quake is estimated to have been around 7.9.

The 1906 earthquake is forever linked with the fires that came after the shaking. About three-fifths of San Francisco was destroyed. The city's population had grown to about 400,000 since the fires of 50 years earlier. The exact number of people who died in this earthquake and the fires may never be known, but most of downtown, the Financial District, Chinatown, Russian Hill, North Beach, the Mission District, and other areas vanished after the 1906 earthquake and fires.

Two downtown buildings, the Montgomery Block and the Parrott Block, stand out for surviving the 1906 earthquake and fires due to their construction and because they had metal shutters preventing the fire from burning all that was inside. The Old Mint at Fifth and Mission Streets also had this feature and survived the 1906 disaster.

Thousands of places in San Francisco also vanished due to various 20th-century earthquakes or fires. Some of those are described in this book, including the 1897 City Hall, the original Beach Chalet, Sweeny's Observatory, Mark Hopkins Institute of Art (and other mansions on Nob Hill), the What Cheer House, Meiggs' Wharf, the Central and Embarcadero Freeways, St. Mary's Cathedral on Van Ness Avenue, Beth Israel Synagogue, and Albert Pike Scottish Rite Temple (later Peoples Temple).

San Francisco is a constantly growing city and often suffers from a housing shortage. Sometimes old buildings are razed to make space for newer, larger ones. Also, land is scarce in San Francisco, so new buildings continue to grow taller to accommodate more living or working spaces.

Development does not always mean tearing down old buildings to build new ones. As the city has grown, people have created new neighborhoods where there was once open space or few buildings. The tony Marina District was developed in this way. In 1915, the Panama-Pacific International Exposition (PPIE) was held on former swampland in the area, then called Harbor View. This land had been unused until the PPIE was built. When the fair was over, the exhibits were razed, and builders developed the land into the Marina District.

In the 1920s, San Francisco builders discovered the empty sand dunes of the Sunset District and, within 30 years, covered its 5.7 square miles with housing and other buildings. In fact, chapter seven shows the Xerces blue butterfly, which disappeared because of all this development. When builders were finished with the Sunset District, some developers moved out of San Francisco south to Daly City and built there.

The development of the Sunset District involved erecting thousands of new buildings without displacing existing ones. What has vanished from these areas are the sand dunes and the views and open land that used to be there. This change continues today with new developments in the Lake Merced area, Mission Bay, and South Beach.

San Francisco built an artificial island in San Francisco Bay to host a major fair, the Golden Gate International Exposition (GGIE), in the late 1930s. Buildings and exhibits were constructed, and when the fair was over in 1940, San Francisco was unable to develop this land. Because of the impending Second World War, the US Navy took over Treasure Island and used it as a base for more than 50 years. The island was given back to San Francisco in 1997. The exhibits that made up the GGIE had been destroyed. Today, one group is working toward creating a new *Pacifica* sculpture (see page 59), but other than that, only a building or two remain from that fair. A new San Francisco neighborhood is being developed on the island.

Other reasons for replacing a building are to create something larger, more modern, safer, or more lucrative. For example, by the time Storyland (which was located in the San Francisco Zoo) closed, interest had declined, while the use of the land as a children's zoo was gaining strength. Parkside School was a K–6 school until the 1970s. It was razed in the early 2000s to build Dianne

Feinstein Elementary School, which had more state-of-the-art modern features. The old Fontana warehouse was replaced by a modern (and lucrative) apartment building that caused an unparalleled view of San Francisco Bay to disappear for thousands of San Franciscans. The 1860s Platt Music Hall was torn down in 1890 and replaced by a large office building that still stands today. The San Francisco approach to the Golden Gate Bridge was unsafe and needed a better roadway, so Doyle Drive was torn down and replaced by the new Presidio Parkway. In the same way, the eastern span of the Bay Bridge still worked but was dangerous, so a new bridge span was built.

The last cause for change has to do with people's interests. The most obvious occasions where these changes come into play are seen in the entertainment industry. For example, people stopped attending movie theaters when they found other things to do (think television). Fleishhacker Pool was once a popular destination, but people stopped going there when they became more mobile and interested in traveling to warmer climates. For similar reasons, over time, fewer people attended Playland-at-the-Beach and Storyland. Customers stopped going to Crystal Palace Market when it was easier to shop at supermarkets in their own neighborhoods. The Chutes amusement park lost its source of customers when people's entertainment interests changed to vaudeville and motion pictures.

The real theme of *Vanished San Francisco* is that cities are always changing. A building is created and—for one or more reasons—is destroyed. Sometimes, as in the case of San Francisco's earthquakes and fires, the loss comes from an act of nature. Other times, things disappear because people's tastes and interests change. When a building, roadway, or source of pleasure vanishes, it might be sorely missed, or people might not even notice that it is gone. In any case, these creations and disappearances are always part of cities that are changing and moving ahead.

One

EARTHQUAKES AND FIRES

In the 1800s, many new San Francisco residents lived in flammable tents and ramshackle wooden houses. Fire became an ever-present danger. Six highly destructive fires burned between December 1849 and June 1851. Each fire destroyed homes and important buildings in the small but greatly populated city. After each fire, people built again and hoped for the best.

Over the years, other fires became famous for destroying buildings around the city. Baldwin's Hotel and Theatre (in 1898), the Cliff House (in 1907), and Sutro Baths (in 1966) disappeared forever due to fires. Other buildings described elsewhere in this book were also destroyed by fire; they are in other chapters related to their uses.

San Francisco is also known for its earthquakes, especially the one that struck at 5:12 a.m. on April 18, 1906. People were shaken out of their beds in one of the best-known disasters of the 20th century. The subsequent fires gutted many of the buildings left standing after the earthquake. The earthquake had destroyed water mains, so the fire department was unable to stop the fires. San Francisco burned for three days. About three-fifths of the small city vanished due to the earthquake and fire. Hundreds, maybe thousands of people were killed, and thousands of residents became homeless.

Living in San Francisco means living with earthquakes—and not knowing when the next one will strike or how destructive it will be. Two smaller earthquakes in 1957 and 1989 reminded San Franciscans that they live in "Earthquake Country."

In the mid-1800s, San Francisco suffered multiple fires in about 18 months. Altogether, about 3,000 structures were destroyed, and the combined damage was $30 million (more than $1 billion today). As soon as each fire ended, people began to rebuild. The first fire started in Dennison's Exchange (above) on Washington Street on December 24, 1849. The second fire (below) began at 4:00 a.m. on May 4, 1850, and burned three blocks of buildings near Portsmouth Square. The third fire broke out on June 14, 1850, causing more damage than either of the first two; the windy day helped spread the fire. More new buildings would be made of bricks, considered to be fire-resistant. Both of these images are from *The Annals of San Francisco*, which was first published in 1855.

The fourth major fire, on September 17, 1850, destroyed more than 150 buildings. The fifth fire (above), on May 4, 1851, was the worst of them all. It destroyed more than 1,000 buildings—three-fourths of the fledgling city. The custom house (below), a large new brick building, could not survive this fire. But that was not the last conflagration. On June 22, 1851, a house on Pacific Avenue burned, starting the sixth fire. It spread quickly, and between 400 and 500 houses were lost. Both of these images are from *The Annals of San Francisco*, which was first published in 1855.

The first Cliff House was built in 1863 at the end of Point Lobos Road. At first, the resort attracted the wealthy elite in San Francisco, but its reputation became shady in the 1870s. Adolph Sutro bought the Cliff House in 1883 and began to restore the building and its reputation. In 1894, before renovations were complete, the Cliff House was destroyed by fire. (Courtesy of Pacific Gas & Electric Co.)

After the first Cliff House burned down, Adolph Sutro spent $75,000 to build an elaborate Victorian-style Cliff House. It was eight stories tall and had turrets, decorative spires, fanciful roof dormers, and an observation tower. It was designed for dining, dancing, and entertainment, and it quickly became a top destination for San Franciscans and visitors. (Courtesy of the San Francisco Department of Public Works.)

San Francisco, California
The world-famed Cliff House

The famous Cliff House
destroyed by fire Sept.
7, 1907.

All that was left of the world-
famed Cliff House after the
fire.

Not everyone liked the Victorian Cliff House. In 1905, city planner Daniel Burnham recommended that the Cliff House be condemned and removed to open the ocean view. Many of Burnham's San Francisco ideas were never implemented, at least partly because of the desire to rebuild quickly after the 1906 earthquake and fire. The Cliff House survived the 1906 disaster but was destroyed by fire in 1907. (Courtesy of Alan Thomas.)

Elias Jackson "Lucky" Baldwin (1828–1909) came to San Francisco in 1853 after becoming wealthy from the silver Comstock Lode in Nevada. He wanted to build a hotel that would attract the elite and compete with the new Palace Hotel. He spent $800,000—more than $18 million in today's money—building the elegant 595-room Baldwin Hotel and Theatre (left) at Market and Powell Streets. Both the hotel and the theater were successful for almost 30 years, but on November 23, 1898, fire destroyed the building, as shown below. The building was underinsured and not rebuilt. Since 1904, the Flood Building, once occupied by the largest store in the Woolworth chain, has stood on this corner. (Both, courtesy of the San Francisco Department of Public Works.)

On April 18, 1906, at 5:12 a.m., San Francisco suffered an event for which it is well known. At that moment, a major earthquake occurred on the San Andreas Fault close to San Francisco. In a 200-mile area around San Francisco, the earthquake shook people from their beds. The ensuing fires killed thousands of people and destroyed thousands of buildings. (Courtesy of the National Archives, photograph no. 2127357.)

Once the ground stopped shaking, people went outside to explore the ruined city. Outside walls were often destroyed, exposing people's private lives. Many people posed for pictures amid the rubble. Close looks at many of these photographs reveal well-dressed people. (Courtesy of the San Francisco Historical Society.)

In 1872, San Francisco began construction of the city hall buildings at Larkin Street near Grove Street. Construction was embroiled in scandal and delays. The city originally announced that the new city hall would open in three years, but the planning and building took 27 years to complete. Shown at left, it finally opened in 1899 and was considered earthquake-resistant. However, in the 1906 earthquake, the building immediately collapsed (below), leaving only the dome intact. After seven years of delays, ground was broken for a new city hall in April 1913. It was completed by 1916 and is still used today. (Both, courtesy of the San Francisco Historical Society.)

In the late 1800s, Thomas Sweeny, who lived just south of Golden Gate Park at Seventh Avenue and Judah Street, donated money for an observatory. The Sweeny Observatory was built in 1891 on the top of Strawberry Hill (named for the wild berries that once grew there). People could see a 360-degree view of San Francisco from the second floor of the observatory. (Courtesy of a private collector.)

Just after the Sweeny Observatory was built in 1891, one published article proclaimed it earthquake-proof. However, when the earthquake struck in 1906, the observatory was destroyed, as shown on this postcard. The Sweeny Observatory was never rebuilt. Since the time of the earthquake, the trees have grown so tall that it is not possible to see much of the city—except downtown skyscrapers—from Strawberry Hill. (Courtesy of John Freeman.)

This view shows the devastation caused by the 1906 earthquake and subsequent fires. The relatively new city hall, which was destroyed by the shaking, is visible in the center of the photograph. Some

buildings fell completely to the ground; others had portions that remained standing. (Courtesy of the San Francisco Historical Society.)

San Francisco might have recovered quickly from the 1906 earthquake if not for the fires. Firefighters could not stop the burning because the earthquake had broken multiple water mains, so the fires continued for more than three days. About 500 blocks were destroyed; property loss totaled more than $350,000 (more than $2 million in 2022 dollars). Hundreds, maybe thousands of people died. (Courtesy of the San Francisco Historical Society.)

This photograph shows a good example of a building that might have survived the 1906 earthquake but was destroyed by fire. The brick walls of the structure remained after the earthquake struck, but the interior and roof were completely overwhelmed by fire, so nothing was left except a brick shell. (Courtesy of the San Francisco Historical Society.)

These two images by photographer Arnold Genthe show fascinated San Francisco residents watching the smoke and fire after the 1906 earthquake. At right, people in Chinatown seem alarmed by the billowing smoke moving closer to them. Below, people on Sacramento Street came out of their damaged homes and watched the conflagration, which must have appeared far away. Eventually, most of downtown was overcome by fire, and by the time it was over, most of the buildings in these two photographs no longer existed. The fire was stopped at Van Ness Avenue, but then it spun northeast to consume most of the neighborhoods of Russian Hill and North Beach. (Both, photograph by Arnold Genthe; courtesy of the Library of Congress.)

A section of the great firestorm following the 1906 earthquake was blamed on a late-riser who tried to cook breakfast on a stove with a damaged flue, sparking the "ham-and-eggs fire." At that point, San Francisco authorities prohibited all cooking indoors until the flues passed a safety inspection. (Courtesy of the San Francisco Historical Society.)

As one woman continues cooking a meal, a group around her on the street poses for a photograph. Many people did not leave their stoves open to the elements but built wooden containers around them. Some even gave them fictitious restaurant names, showing that a sense of humor survived the tragedy. (Courtesy of the National Archives, photograph no. 2127314.)

Mark Hopkins began building his elaborate mansion on San Francisco's Nob Hill in 1875, but he died in 1878 before the mansion was finished. The huge building on Nob Hill was eventually donated to the University of California for art instruction, and it became the Mark Hopkins Institute of Art. (Courtesy of OpenSFHistory, wnp13.077.)

The Mark Hopkins Institute of Art (forerunner of the San Francisco Institute of Art) burned to the ground after the 1906 earthquake. This image shows people walking toward the top of Nob Hill, perhaps to see the remains of the Mark Hopkins mansion, whose tower remains upright at the top of the hill. The Mark Hopkins Hotel now stands on the site. (Courtesy of the Library of Congress.)

A lot of places that survived the 1906 earthquake were later destroyed by fire. After the fires were out, many areas showed only desolation. In these two photographs, the fire has clearly caused entire areas to disappear. Some chimneys and building frames remain standing, indicating that the fire burned all that was flammable. Because fires were more familiar (and perhaps more seemingly controllable) to people than an earthquake, for many years, city promoters talked about the fire of 1906, not the earthquake, fearing they might frighten tourists away from visiting San Francisco or discourage businesses from investing in the city. (Above, courtesy of the San Francisco Historical Society; below, courtesy of the Library of Congress.)

Large numbers of people walked to the Ferry Building, which is visible in the smoke in the distant background of this photograph. Many people fled San Francisco on the free ferry service provided by Southern Pacific. Some sought temporary respite in the East Bay but returned when conditions improved in San Francisco. Others stayed with friends or family outside the city and may have never returned. (Courtesy of the Library of Congress.)

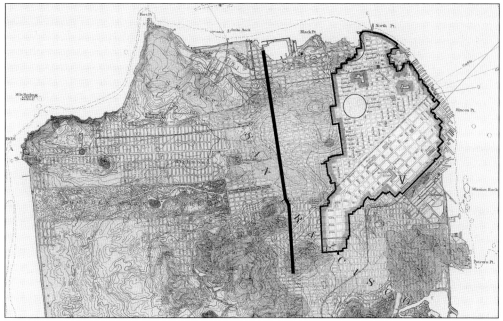

More than three-fifths of San Francisco was destroyed by the earthquake and fire. Today's seven square miles of San Francisco are completely developed, but in 1906, almost all houses and businesses stood to the right (east) of the vertical black line on this map. The outlined area, which marks what was burned during the 1906 fires, makes it clear that more than half of the city was destroyed. This map was created by Chris Carlsson.

After the 1906 disaster, many refugees lived in tents, but as winter grew near, people worried about the oncoming rainy season. More than 5,600 one-room cottages were built and placed on open land around the city. Pictured are some of the 4,130 people who lived in Camp Richmond, the largest site. Few earthquake cottages remain, although one of them is a city landmark in the Sunset District. (Courtesy of Alan Thomas.)

In 1906, earthquake cottages were set up in what had been Jewish cemeteries (until 1865) at Eighteenth and Dolores Streets. In 1905, the area became Dolores Park, and by late April 1906, it was a tent camp. The building in the background is the original Mission High School, which was constructed in 1896 and burned down in 1922. (Courtesy of San Jose State University Special Collections & Archives.)

The story of St. Mary's Cathedral of the Assumption in San Francisco is about three buildings, two of which still stand. The original 1854 St. Mary's, on California Street at Grant Avenue, still offers services. The second St. Mary's (right) opened on Van Ness Avenue in 1891 and was destroyed by fire in 1962. A new St. Mary's (below) opened at 1111 Gough Street in 1971 and still stands. This cathedral is much different from its predecessors. Because of its modern look, newspaper columnist Herb Caen labeled it "Our Lady of Maytag" and "the washing machine agitator"—a description that sticks to this day. (Right, courtesy of the San Francisco History Center, San Francisco Public Library; below, photograph by Ron Henggeler.)

St. Paulus Lutheran Church (pictured at left) was built in 1893 on Eddy Street at Gough Street. The church served as a shelter and hospital for victims of the 1906 earthquake and fire. In 1995, the church burned down. In January 2010, St. Paulus lent one third of an acre of unused land to Free Farm (below), an organization in which volunteers tend crops and distribute free organic produce to low-income individuals and families. In 2013, the farm was abandoned when construction began on an apartment building on the lot. St. Paulus does not have a new building, but it is still holding services and continuing its social outreach mission. (Left, courtesy of the San Francisco History Center, San Francisco Public Library; below, photograph by Chris Carlsson.)

The original Beach Chalet opened in 1892 on the beach side of the Great Highway. It contained a snack bar, an observation deck, a reading room, and changing rooms. A strong storm in 1914 undermined the building, which was moved to Twenty-Fourth Avenue and used as a Boy Scout troop clubhouse. It was destroyed by fire in 1958. (Courtesy of the San Francisco Department of Public Works.)

Wealthy San Franciscan Andrew McCreery donated $50,000 to build the McCreery Branch public library, one of only two branches named after donors. Opened in 1903, the library survived the 1906 earthquake, but it was damaged by the 1957 earthquake and had to be razed. It was replaced by the Eureka Valley Branch Library, also called the Harvey Milk Memorial Library. (Courtesy of the San Francisco History Center, San Francisco Public Library.)

While San Francisco's "freeway revolt" of the 1950s and 1960s crushed many planned freeways around the city, the Embarcadero Freeway (above) was one of the few projects that went through. Opened in 1959, Freeway 480 cast a shadow on the iconic Ferry Building and cut off the plaza from walkers and drivers. The final scene in the 1958 film *The Lineup* features this freeway just before it opened. Many people argued for razing the ugly freeway; others liked its easy access to Chinatown and North Beach. The 1989 earthquake severely damaged the Embarcadero Freeway, and it was torn down in 1991 (left). (Above, courtesy of the San Francisco History Center, San Francisco Public Library; left, photograph by Greg Gaar.)

Oakland's "Cypress Structure," a double-decker section of Highway 880, was built in the 1950s. During the 1989 Loma Prieta earthquake, the top roadway pancaked onto the roadway below it, killing 42 people. This highway section was later torn down and replaced by a single-decker freeway. (Photograph by David Coteur; courtesy of the San Francisco History Center, San Francisco Public Library.)

Many buildings sustained major damage in the 1989 Loma Prieta earthquake, which was the strongest earthquake to hit the San Francisco Bay Area since 1906. This apartment building on the northwest corner of Seventh Avenue and Judah Street did not collapse, but it was so badly damaged that the owner decided to tear it down and construct a new apartment building. (Photograph by the author.)

This 1989 photograph shows three important buildings, two of which no longer exist. On the far left, the Fillmore Auditorium, famous for music in the late 1960s, still stands. The building next to it was once the Beth Israel Synagogue and later held art by designer Tony Duquette. It was destroyed by fire in 1989. On the right stood the Albert Pike Scottish Rite Temple, later the center of Jim Jones's Peoples Temple until 1977. The 1989 earthquake damaged these two buildings, which were torn down and replaced by a post office. (Photograph by Greg Gaar.)

Two

TRANSPORTATION

Getting to and around San Francisco has always been a challenge. After gold was discovered at Sutter's Mill in 1848, people came from all over the world to make their fortunes. Some became rich; many did not.

In the early days, most people traveled to San Francisco by ship. A familiar sight in San Francisco Bay during the California Gold Rush was the great number of abandoned ships. Immediately upon arriving in San Francisco, travelers and crews left for gold country. Some of these ships were used as buildings in the growing city; others become buried under new structures as the bay was filled with land that expanded the city's coastline.

Between San Francisco's steep hills and the sand on which most structures were built, getting around the city in the early years was difficult. For example, the expensive area known as Nob Hill had few residents because the hills were too steep for horses to safely traverse them. This changed with the invention of the cable car, and many wealthy people began to build their mansions atop Nob Hill. In another example, the western part of San Francisco was filled with sand dunes that were deeper than in other areas of the city. Development was slow, but once the Sunset District and Twin Peaks streetcar tunnels were built, the neighborhoods grew quickly.

Ships, horses, streetcars, cable cars, trains, buses, and automobiles have all been involved in transportation in San Francisco. The city is unique in how it has reused transportation methods. Early in San Francisco's history, ships were used as buildings. Obsolete streetcars and cable cars became meeting places and homes near the beach. A retired locomotive and an old Navy jet even provided climbing opportunities for children.

When gold was discovered in California in 1848, men came from all over world hoping to make their fortunes. Much of San Francisco Bay was covered with ships that had been deserted by

both passengers and crews. When areas of the bay were later filled in, the ships were buried under buildings. (Courtesy of the Library of Congress.)

Niantic was a whaling ship that brought gold-seekers to San Francisco in 1849. The passengers and most of the crew abandoned *Niantic* to go to the goldfields, and it was run aground at what is now the intersection of Clay and Sansome Streets. The upper part of the ship burned during the fire of May 4, 1851. Later, the Niantic Hotel burned in the 1906 disaster. Artifacts and the ship's log were excavated in 1978 and are on display at the San Francisco Maritime Museum. The *Euphemia* (below), abandoned in San Francisco Bay at Battery Street, served as a floating jail from 1849 to 1851, when a jail building opened. As the bay was filled in, the ship was buried; it was rediscovered during construction in 1921. (Both, courtesy of the Library of Congress.)

San Francisco's original Ferry Building (above) was constructed in 1880. It was torn down and replaced in 1898 by the current Ferry Building (below), designed by A.P. Brown. This Ferry Building still stands, but the pedestrian footbridge (Embarcadero Overpass) is gone. This cast-iron walkway allowed pedestrians entering and exiting the Ferry Building to avoid the surface streets crowded with local streetcars and automobiles. The Embarcadero Overpass was removed around 1942 to be used as scrap metal during World War II and was never rebuilt. Streetcars no longer stop at the Ferry Building, and the opening of the bridges greatly reduced ferry traffic, so a pedestrian overpass is no longer needed. (Above, courtesy of Pacific Gas & Electric Co.; below, courtesy of the San Francisco Department of Public Works.)

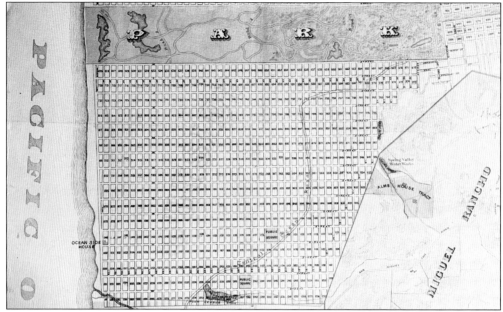

This 1879 map shows the now-familiar grid layout in the Sunset District, but until the 1920s, the only road running through the Sunset was the winding Central Ocean Macadamized Toll Road built in 1864. For many years, the only ways in and out of the Sunset were from the north or south or via the Central Ocean Road. (Courtesy of Dennis Minnick.)

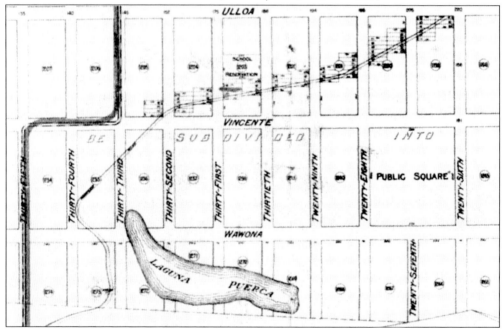

The Parkside Realty Company began building homes in 1908. It had to orient houses so they would fit on the gridded streets shown on this 1870 map, even though none of these streets yet existed. This map of homes for sale shows the houses clustered around the Central Ocean Macadamized Toll Road. The road no longer exists, and the surviving houses fit the grid. (Courtesy of the Western Neighborhoods Project.)

In December 1883, Southern Pacific opened the Park and Ocean Railroad, running a steam train from Haight and Stanyan Streets along H Street (now Lincoln Way) to 49th Avenue. The round trip took 20 minutes. In 1899, streetcars replaced the trains, and in 1948, buses replaced the streetcars. (Courtesy of the San Francisco History Center, San Francisco Public Library.)

In 1902, streetcars began running on H Street (now Lincoln Way). Not many people lived by the beach, but visitors to the Cliff House (page 14), Sutro Baths (page 74), and later Playland (page 82) rode this streetcar to the beach to get closer to those destinations. Streetcars disappeared from Lincoln Way in the 1940s, when most streetcar lines were changed to diesel bus lines. (Courtesy of Emiliano Echeverria.)

One of the main north–south streets in San Francisco is Nineteenth Avenue, a six-lane road that carries more than 50,000 cars each day. Here is the road in 1900. When development began in the Sunset District in the 1920s, Nineteenth Avenue was a two-lane road. It was widened to six lanes in 1937 to provide a quicker route to the new Golden Gate Bridge. (Courtesy of a private collector.)

Sunset District development was hindered by the lack of public transportation. The first streetcar line operated from 1908 to 1945 and ran on Twentieth Avenue between Ulloa Street and Lincoln Way, so passengers could transfer to a streetcar headed downtown. The line was planned for Nineteenth Avenue, but Twentieth Avenue had less traffic, so the tracks could be laid more easily. Today, no public transportation line runs on Twentieth Avenue. (Courtesy of Emiliano Echeverria.)

Point Lobos Toll Road was built in the early 1860s so people could travel through the fledgling Richmond District to the Cliff House and Sutro Baths. In 1863, Mark Twain wrote about traveling on this road: "The wind was cold and benumbing, and . . . came straight from the ocean. . . . I think there are icebergs out there somewhere." This photograph was taken in 1880. (Courtesy of a private collector.)

This image shows the busy Southern Pacific train depot at Third and Townsend Streets in 1948. Designed in the Mission Revival style, it opened in 1915 to serve people attending the Panama-Pacific International Exhibition (see page 56). By 1971, train travel had declined, and lines were cut or moved to Oakland. The depot was razed in 1976, when a smaller terminal opened at Fourth and King Streets. (Courtesy of Jack Tillmany.)

In the late 1800s, Market Street Railway Company owned the block bounded by Lincoln Way, Funston Avenue, Irving Street, and Fourteenth Avenue. The company planned to build a carbarn (a place where streetcars were repaired), but that never happened. Instead, it became a place where old streetcars "went to die" and was known as the Boneyard (above and below). One man remembers that as a boy, he looked for streetcars with unlocked doors; he would sit in the driver's seat and pretend that he was driving. In the early 1940s, the Boneyard was replaced by a grocery store and an apartment complex. (Above, courtesy of Emiliano Echeverria; below, courtesy of Jack Tillmany.)

In 1913, transportation expert Bion J. Arnold wrote that outlying neighborhoods would never grow until it took 30 minutes or less to travel downtown. The two-mile Twin Peaks tunnel opened in 1918, running streetcars that linked the Sunset District with downtown. The tunnel still stands today, but in the 1970s, it was revamped for new streetcars, and the original 1917 Beaux-Arts entrance at the west portal was replaced. (Courtesy of a private collector.)

When the San Francisco–Oakland Bay Bridge opened in 1936, cars drove in both directions on the top deck. Buses, large trucks, and Key System commuter trains traveled on the lower deck. The Key System closed in 1960; since 1963, the bottom deck has carried all traffic going east (out of San Francisco), while the upper deck is one-way west (into the city). (Courtesy of the San Francisco Department of Public Works.)

Lombard Street, shown here in a view looking west from Leavenworth Street to Hyde Street, was once a steep country road. Because of the 27-degree grade, the "Crookedest Street in the World" was created in 1922. The *Guinness Book of World Records* defines "Little Lombard" as the crookedest street, but measurements show that San Francisco's Vermont Street has steeper curves. (Courtesy of the San Francisco Department of Public Works.)

For years, El Camino del Mar linked the Legion of Honor Museum with Point Lobos, located above the Cliff House. Built on unstable ground, the road often washed out during winter storms. It was permanently closed in the 1950s and is now part of a hiking path for walkers only. (Courtesy of the San Francisco History Center, San Francisco Public Library.)

The 1989 Loma Prieta earthquake damaged one of San Francisco's major roadways, the Central Freeway (above). A decision was made to raze the freeway, build new housing, and expand Octavia Street into a boulevard with green space. For 20 years after the earthquake, an empty lot sat under the old Central Freeway at 450 Laguna Street. In January 2010, San Francisco activated this lot for temporary use as a green space (below). Thousands of people volunteered to transform it into an area with fruit forests, bio-intensive cultivation practices, and community gathering spaces. Although the lot was developed into condominiums within a few years, for a short time, it was the Hayes Valley Farm. (Above, courtesy of the San Francisco History Center, San Francisco Public Library; below, photograph by Chris Carlsson.)

As the Golden Gate Bridge was being built, Doyle Drive was constructed to connect San Francisco with the bridge. Built in 1936, Doyle Drive was an elevated highway approximately 1.6 miles in length. Much of the six-lane Doyle Drive was dangerous. Nothing separated the three lanes of cars driving in one direction from the three lanes driving in the opposite direction, and serious head-on collisions occurred over the years. The unsafe road was also especially vulnerable to

earthquakes. It was damaged in the 1989 earthquake, and some repairs were made, but by the early 2000s, federal highway officials gave the road a safety rating of 2 out of 100. Doyle Drive was torn down and replaced by the ground-level Presidio Parkway, which opened in 2015. (Courtesy of Bancroft Library.)

The San Francisco–Oakland Bay Bridge opened in 1936. The bridge is made up of two separate spans: a suspension bridge that runs from San Francisco to Yerba Island (the western span) and a cantilever bridge, shown here, from the island to Oakland (the eastern span). In the 1989 earthquake, a section of the eastern span roadway collapsed onto the lower deck of the bridge. The newly built eastern span opened in September 2013. (Photograph by Ron Henggeler.)

Starting in 1959, three decommissioned Navy jets took turns sitting at Larsen Park. Children climbed over them, sat in the cockpits, and jumped to the ground from high spots. When children wore out the first jet, it was removed and replaced by another. A third jet was removed in 1993 and not replaced. In 2015, a sculpted replica of a jet arrived to entertain a new generation. (Courtesy of Richard Lim.)

Three

WORLD FAIRS

San Francisco hosted three distinct fairs and expositions in the years between 1894 and 1940. As with most fairs, the exhibits were beautiful and extravagant but temporary—they vanished when the fair ended. A few exceptions remain, but generally, none of the exhibits were preserved after each fair ended.

The California Midwinter Exposition, usually called the 1894 Midwinter Fair, was held in Golden Gate Park from January 27 to July 5, 1894. Many of the exhibits came from the World's Columbian Exposition held in Chicago in 1893. Historians estimate that more than two million people attended this fair. The Japanese Tea Garden began at this fair and survives today, although none of the exhibits from the original fair remain in the garden. The land on which the fair exhibits were built is now the Music Concourse, which is set aside for live concerts and surrounded by the major park buildings.

The Panama–Pacific International Exposition (PPIE) was held from February 20 to December 14, 1915, on 636 acres that later became the Marina District neighborhood. The fair's purpose was to celebrate the completion of the Panama Canal and highlight the achievements of East and West together. However, San Franciscans also used it to show that the city had recovered from the 1906 disaster. Almost 19 million people attended this fair. The Palace of Fine Arts, rebuilt and remodeled several times, is the only survivor from the PPIE.

About 10 million people attended the last fair held in San Francisco, the Golden Gate International Exposition (GGIE). It opened on February 18 and closed on September 29, 1939. But after calls to open it again, it reopened from May 25 to September 29, 1940. One of the main reasons for the fair was to celebrate the two San Francisco bridges built and opened in the mid-1930s: the San Francisco–Oakland Bay Bridge (1936) and the Golden Gate Bridge (1937). The GGIE was held on Treasure Island, a man-made island created for the fair. The celebrations became bittersweet as World War II approached, and some foreign exhibits closed early because of war activities.

On August 24, 1893, more than 50,000 people attended the ground-breaking event for the 1894 California Midwinter International Exposition in Golden Gate Park. More than 100 buildings were built on 200 acres, and the fair opened on January 27, 1894. Estimates say that more than two million people attended the fair before it closed on July 4. (Courtesy of a private collector.)

The bright light of the tower at night was a striking part of the Midwinter Fair. Park superintendent John McLaren only begrudgingly accepted a temporary fair. Popular lore says that McLaren became impatient with the city for not removing the tower 18 months after the fair ended and gave park gardeners dynamite to blow it up. (Courtesy of the San Francisco History Center, San Francisco Public Library.)

Many buildings at the Midwinter Fair featured foreign exhibits, but the Agricultural and Horticulture Building was primarily a showcase of what could be raised and harvested in California. It stood on the north side of Golden Gate Park's Music Concourse, and it cost $58,500 to build. (Photograph by I.W. Taber; courtesy of the Library of Congress.)

One exhibit built for the Midwinter Fair that still thrives today is the Japanese Tea Garden. George Turner Marsh, a collector of Japanese art, designed the original Japanese Village; Makoto Hagiwara transformed the exhibit into the Japanese Tea Garden and ran it for many years. The famous Chinese fortune cookie originated in the Japanese Village at the Midwinter Fair. (Courtesy of the San Francisco History Center, San Francisco Public Library.)

Two amusement rides were popular at the Midwinter Fair. The Firth Wheel was a smaller version of the Ferris wheel, a huge moneymaker at the 1893 World's Columbian Exposition in Chicago. The Ferris wheel was not available, so the Midwinter Fair committee negotiated with J. Kirk Firth to design and build a half-scale version of it. The Firth Wheel was put on a riser, so its apex was 73 feet taller than the Ferris wheel, providing riders with a great view. The other ride was the Haunted Swing (left), which used an optical illusion to startle riders. People sat on a large stationary swing while the scenery on the surrounding walls, floor, and ceiling moved around, making riders think the swing itself went in a complete circle. (Above, courtesy of the Library of Congress; left, public domain.)

The stereographic image above shows the Fine Arts Building, constructed to display exhibits at the Midwinter Fair. Following the exposition, the building was designated as a museum for the people of San Francisco. The chair of the fair's organizing committee was Michael H. de Young, cofounder of the *San Francisco Chronicle*. A new museum (below) was built and opened in Golden Gate Park in 1919. It was named the M.H. de Young Memorial Museum to honor his extensive work on the Midwinter Fair. This museum served San Francisco until the end of 2000, when it was torn down and replaced by a more modern building. (Above, courtesy of the Library of Congress; below, courtesy of the San Francisco Historical Society.)

The 1915 Panama-Pacific International Exhibition (PPIE) was held on swampy land in northern San Francisco. The advertised purpose was to celebrate the 1914 completion of the Panama Canal, but a major goal was to promote tourism and investment by showing that San Francisco had recovered from the disaster of 1906. After the fair, most exhibits were torn down, and the land was developed into the Marina District. (Courtesy of the San Francisco Archives.)

The Court of the Universe was the largest and grandest court at the PPIE. The two triumphal arches represented the nations of the East meeting the nations of the West—a concept people seemed to embrace with the opening of the Panama Canal. The Tower of Jewels, at left, had more than 100,000 cut jewels that sparkled in daylight and 50 spotlights that illuminated it at night. (Courtesy of James Smith.)

When the PPIE ended, San Francisco planned to develop the marshland on which it was built into a residential area: the new Marina District. The Preservation League wanted to save three buildings: the Palace of Fine Arts (left), the 185-foot-high Column of Progress (center), and the California Counties Building (right). The only building saved was the Palace of Fine Arts, designed by architect Bernard Maybeck. (Courtesy of the San Francisco Department of Public Works.)

According to the National Park Service, "the Palace of Fine Arts was widely considered the greatest of the palaces, in both appearance and substance. More than half of the visitors on any given day visited it; and by the end of the Exposition, at least ten million people." The palace still stands today and is the only remaining exhibit from the PPIE. (Photograph by Ron Henggeler.)

Treasure Island in San Francisco Bay is a man-made island created for the Golden Gate International Exposition (above). About 10 million people attended this fair in San Francisco, which was open from February 18 to September 29, 1939. It reopened from May 25 to September 29, 1940, as Cavalcade of Music. After the fair ended, the island was taken over by the US Navy for World War II operations. The island still exists—as well as one or two buildings from the exposition—but the exhibits were torn down when the fair ended. When the Loma Prieta earthquake hit in 1989, some of the exhibits, including the Tower of the Sun (left), partially appeared above ground when the island sank during liquefaction. (Above, courtesy of the San Francisco Department of Public Works; left, courtesy of the *San Francisco Chronicle*.)

The above photograph, which was remastered and preserved by Ron Henggeler, shows the Golden Gate International Exposition's Court of Reflections as seen from the top of the Tower of the Sun. Pictured below is the creation of sculptor Ralph Stackpole, the 80-foot-tall *Pacifica*, the largest statue at the exposition. It was lit by two 1,500-watt underwater floodlights. The fountain in front was surrounded with sculptures representing people living on the shores of the Pacific. *Pacifica* was demolished by the US Navy on January 22, 1941. (Above, photograph by Marcello Camarri; below, photograph by Karl Jacob, courtesy of P. Carpenter and P. Totah.)

One of the many souvenirs created for the Golden Gate International Exposition was this ashtray showing some of the fair's exhibits. The logo for the fair, reproduced in the center of the ashtray, shows the Tower of the Sun, part of the Bay Bridge, and the year the fair opened. The surrounding images show some of the exhibits. The ashtrays still exist, but the exhibits are long gone. (Photograph by the author.)

Four

FOOD AND DRINK

The most obvious choice for a chapter on food and drink is to delve into the histories of the many outstanding, famous, and quirky restaurants that have disappeared from the San Francisco restaurant scene over the years. It would be difficult to decide which restaurants to highlight and which to omit. Instead, chapter four looks at the unusual.

How and where San Franciscans buy food to take home tells a lot about how people live. In the early 1920s, farmer's markets were gaining ground, as people were discouraged by prices at grocery stores. Many small farmer's markets opened in San Francisco's downtown and residential neighborhoods, although many disappeared when the Crystal Palace Market (CPM) opened at Eighth and Market Streets in 1922. The 70 or so vendors in this 70,000-square-foot building did sell produce, meats, poultry, and cheese to people at reduced prices, but the CPM also had vendors selling products that consumers were not accustomed to seeing, like yogurt ("cultured milk from Bulgaria"), "steamed beer," and New Zealand beef.

The Colombo Market, which began in the late 1800s, was part of the huge downtown produce district. It was not a market for consumers. Instead, farmers brought their produce to the Columbo Market to sell it to those who sold directly to restaurants and consumers. An important industry disappeared when the produce district was replaced by the Golden Gateway redevelopment project in the 1960s.

Of course, the "drink" part of this chapter's title refers to unusual drinking establishments as well. Abe Warner's Cobweb Palace was known for its food and drink but was infamous for the live animals running around and cobwebs covering the furniture and ceilings. An area of the Richmond District became known as Beertown when it became populated with many drinking establishments after a horse-racing track opened nearby. When the racetrack closed, so did much of Beertown.

Abe Warner's Cobweb Palace, a most unusual bar/restaurant, opened on Meiggs' Wharf in 1856. The food and drink were popular, and unusual objects—as well as live monkeys, parrots, and other animals—were visible throughout the building. The most intriguing attraction, though, was the cobwebs (below). Warner (pictured at left) never destroyed a spiderweb, and the results were awe-inspiring. However, by 1893, business had declined, and Warner sold the place. The new owner immediately tore down the building. The Cobweb Palace stood at what is now the north side of Francisco Street midway between Powell and Mason Streets. (Left, courtesy of James Smith; below, courtesy of the San Francisco History Center, San Francisco Public Library.)

In the early 1900s, Carl Larsen's chicken ranch sat on the block between Sixteenth and Seventeenth Avenues and Moraga and Noriega Streets in the undeveloped Sunset District. In the above view looking northwest, the Central Ocean Macadamized Toll Road (see page 40) is west of the ranch, and Golden Gate Park is the long black area at upper right. Below, workers at Larsen's ranch watch the chickens. Larsen lived downtown and owned the Tivoli Café on Eddy Street. Each morning, a horse-drawn carriage took eggs from the chicken ranch to the Tivoli, whose advertisements boasted, "Fresh eggs from Sunset Ranch EVERY DAY." No sign of the ranch or the sand dunes can be seen today. (Above, courtesy of a private collector; below, courtesy of Phil Milholton.)

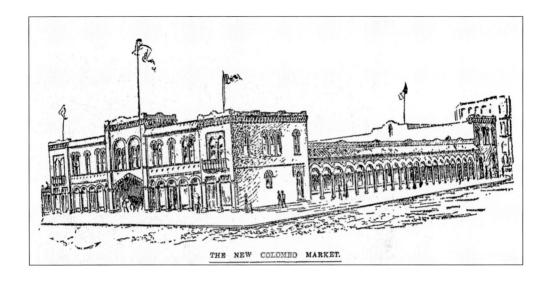

THE NEW COLOMBO MARKET.

The Columbo Market was built in 1874 on Front Street near Jackson Street. It was replaced in 1894 by a building (above) designed by Clinton Day. Colombo was one of San Francisco's largest produce markets for many years. Farmers, mostly native Italians, would bring their goods to the market and sell them to restaurants and purveyors. The market was heavily damaged in the 1906 earthquake but was later rebuilt and operated until 1963. The below photograph shows the market in 1959. The 1949 movie *Thieves' Highway* was filmed in the produce district near the Colombo Market. (Above, courtesy of the *San Francisco Chronicle*; below, courtesy of OpenSFHistory, wnp28.2474.)

In the 1960s, the San Francisco Redevelopment Agency demolished the Colombo Market and the produce district to build a redevelopment agency project, the Golden Gateway. The original arch from the main entrance to the market was saved and now serves as a portal to the Sydney Walton Park on Front Street. The arch is all that remains of Colombo Market. (Photograph by the author.)

In 1874, when the Bay District Racing Track (see page 86) opened on D (now Fulton) Street from First to Fifth Avenues, many saloons began to appear on that five-block stretch of D Street. Soon, the area was dubbed Beertown because of the large number of establishments attracting horse-racing patrons. When the racetrack closed in 1896, the saloons began to disappear, and there is no sign of them today. (Courtesy of a private collector.)

The Crystal Palace Market opened on Eighth and Market Streets in 1922 in a location that was considered to be on the outskirts of San Francisco. By the time the above picture was taken in January 1927, the area was much busier with streetcars, automobiles, and pedestrians. Many movie theaters were nearby, and people often stopped at the market after seeing a film. Inside the Crystal Palace Market (below), 70 or more vendors, always ready to meet and attract new customers, were stacking their shelves high or offering all kinds of specialty foods. (Above, courtesy of the San Francisco History Center, San Francisco Public Library; below, courtesy of Thomas Gille.)

Doggie Diner (above) was a fast-food place known for its mascot, a seven-foot-tall dachshund head made of red fiberglass. The first Doggie Diner opened in Oakland in 1948, and at its height of popularity, the Bay Area chain boasted 30 outlets. The chain closed forever in 1986. However, people were not ready to let it go. The City and County of San Francisco declared the Doggie Diner head a city landmark on July 7, 1999. In 2012, one of the dog heads was put on a pole and installed on Sloat Boulevard (right) near where one of the last Doggie Diners operated. (Above, photograph by Dennis O'Rorke; right, photograph by the author.)

In the early 1900s, the Fontana pasta factory (above), which was later used for offices and food storage, stood on North Point Street between Polk Street and Van Ness Avenue. In 1962, long after the Fontana had been demolished, developers built the Fontana Apartments (below), two 17-story buildings, on the site, eliminating the broad view of the San Francisco Bay. The apartments still stand, but the unparalleled view has vanished for anyone who does not live in them. The construction of the apartment buildings spurred action by San Franciscans to set height and other limits on development along the northern shoreline. (Above, courtesy of OpenSFHistory, Marilyn Blaisdell Collection, wnp37.10073; below, photograph by Chris Carlsson.)

The first Mels (originally spelled without an apostrophe) Drive-In restaurant, which is pictured here, opened at 140 South Van Ness Avenue in 1947. Drive-in restaurants were just catching on, and this was the first one in San Francisco. The scenes of "Burger City" in the 1973 movie *American Graffiti* were filmed at this location. There are still seven Mel's restaurants in California, but the original one closed and was torn down in 1976. (Courtesy of the San Francisco History Center, San Francisco Public Library.)

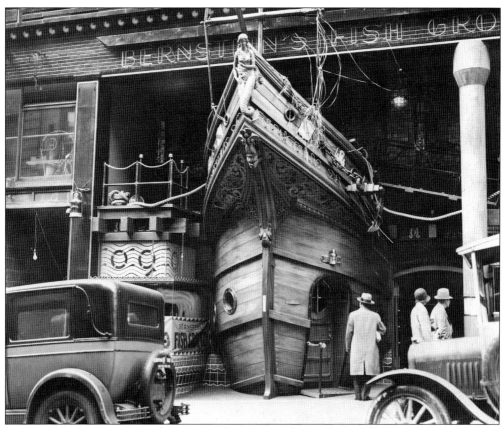

Bernstein's Fish Grotto, located at 123 Powell Street, was known for its fish menu and its re-creation of the prow of Christopher Columbus's ship the *Niña* that jutted out onto the sidewalk. Maurice Bernstein opened the restaurant on the Embarcadero in 1889 and moved it to Powell Street in 1907. After being managed by generations of the Bernstein family, Bernstein's Fish Grotto closed in 1986 and was later torn down. (Courtesy of the San Francisco History Center, San Francisco Public Library.)

In 1895, Dominic Roberts came to San Francisco from Malta. He bought the Sea Breeze resort in the far western part of the city in 1897 and renamed it Roberts Family Resort. Dominic loved to cook and often held popular "bear barbecues," so named for a bear he kept on a collar and chain. Dominic's son Richie ("Shorty") took over Roberts Family Resort after his father died in 1912. When a customer claimed horses could not swim, Shorty made a $1,000 bet that his 12-year-old horse Blackie could swim the bay. Blackie won the bet, swimming from Lime Point in Marin County to Crissy Field in 23 minutes. The 1938 photograph below shows Blackie in the water with Shorty holding onto the horse's tail. (Both, courtesy of Alex Spotorno.)

Five

ENTERTAINMENT

San Francisco has hosted many places where people could go to have fun: Woodward's Gardens, Sutro Baths, Fleishhacker Pool, Chutes amusement parks, Fleishhacker Zoo, Playland-at-the-Beach, and more. These destinations and others existed in San Francisco in the late 1800s and early 1900s. They started to disappear when people began to travel outside the city for their fun.

The San Francisco Zoo still attracts crowds, but the zoo had some amusements that have disappeared over the years—in some cases, when they were replaced by other, more popular attractions.

One of San Francisco's most famous citizens, Adolph Sutro, was famous for the amusement venues he built and operated. He lived on a bluff overlooking the original Cliff House, which he had purchased. When that building burned down, Sutro built a huge Victorian-style Cliff House that is famous to this day, even though it was gone after 1907. He also built Sutro Baths, a huge recreational center along the ocean. It featured seven swimming pools filled with ocean water, with each pool heated to a different temperature. It also included restaurants and an amphitheater. Upstairs, the Sutro Baths Museum exhibited many items Sutro had collected in his extensive travels.

An entire book could be written on the number of movie theaters that once operated in San Francisco but no longer exist. Three are highlighted in this book—the grand Fox Theatre, the largest and most opulent; the Coronet, a neighborhood theater that broke the mold and showed first-run movies; and the Galaxy, the modern attempt to attract a disappearing clientele.

Entertainment also includes sports, and San Francisco's weather generally allows for year-round outdoor events. A number of sports venues that once existed have disappeared. This chapter talks about four stadiums for football and/or baseball. One had a short run, but the other three entertained fans for years.

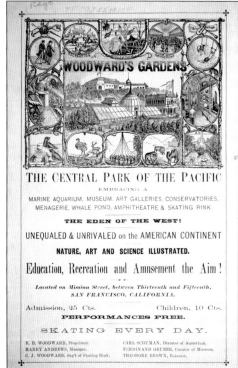

In 1866, Robert B. Woodward converted his four-acre estate between Mission and Valencia Streets and Thirteenth and Fifteenth Streets to Woodward's Gardens (above), which turned into the largest and most popular amusement ground in San Francisco. His home became the Museum of Natural Wonders, holding stuffed bears, birds, fish, fossils, and mineral specimens. Other features of Woodward's Gardens included a conservatory, art gallery, zoo, amphitheater, and ice-skating rink, as well as fountains, streams, small lakes, hillocks, and man-made grottos and caverns. On the poster at left, Woodward called his amusement park "The Central Park of the Pacific" and "The Eden of the West." Woodward died in 1879, and Woodward's Gardens struggled to stay open, but with no leader who shared Woodward's vision, the gardens ended up closing in 1891. In 1893, the land was subdivided and sold. (Above, courtesy of the Library of Congress; left, courtesy of the Sutro Library Branch, California State Library.)

Charles Ackerman opened the Chutes amusement park on Haight Street (above) on November 2, 1895. Passengers climbed onto a boat at the top of a 70-foot-high inclined ramp, rode down 300 feet, and splashed in a pond below. Chutes also had thrill rides, a zoo, and a theater. Two months after Chutes closed in March 1902, Ackerman opened a larger Chutes on Fulton Street at Tenth Avenue (below). The new Chutes had a larger theater, more amusements, and an improved zoo. Charles Ackerman died in January 1909, and his son Irving opened a Chutes on Fillmore Street on July 14, 1909; this Chutes burned down on May 29, 1911. Housing or businesses now stand where all three Chutes once operated. (Both, courtesy of John Freeman.)

Pictured above is a collection of places that stood during Adolph Sutro's lifetime but are now gone. At upper left is his home, which was torn down in 1938. At upper right is the Victorian-style Cliff House that Sutro built in 1896; it burned down in 1907. In 1896, Adolph Sutro opened Sutro Baths, a huge facility that was popular for many years. The exterior of the building is shown in the foreground of the above image, and the interior is pictured below. Swimmers enjoyed seven pools at differing temperatures, plus slides, trapezes, springboards, and a high dive. The baths could accommodate 10,000 people at one time. In 1952, new owners covered the pools with an ice-skating rink. Sutro Baths closed in 1966 and burned down later that year. (Above, courtesy of a private collector; below, courtesy of Marilyn Blaisdell.)

Upstairs from the pools, Adolph Sutro displayed items he had collected over many years, including stuffed and mounted animals, historical artifacts, and mummies. When George Whitney bought the baths in 1952, he added items from his collection. Sutro Baths also had a 2,700-seat amphitheater, clubrooms, and 517 private dressing rooms. The 1958 movie *The Lineup* includes a scene that was filmed inside the Sutro Baths building. (Courtesy of Marilyn Blaisdell.)

The Sutro Baths ruins have fascinated people for many years. When the City of San Francisco controlled the land, it tried to keep people away from the ruins. The area is now owned by the Golden Gate Recreational Area (National Park Service) and is open to the public. A scene in the 1971 movie *Harold and Maude* was filmed among the ruins. (Photograph by the author.)

When Fleishhacker Pool opened in 1925, it was one of the longest outdoor swimming pools in the world. It was so large that lifeguards patrolled in rowboats. It held six million gallons of water pumped in from the nearby Pacific Ocean. The pool closed in 1971, and the San Francisco Zoo parking lot now covers the land where the pool once stood. (Courtesy of a private collector.)

This aerial view of Fleishhacker Pool shows how large it was in relation to its surroundings on the southwest edge of San Francisco. This area of San Francisco is notoriously cold and foggy in the summer, yet the pool was popular for many years. The pool was supposedly heated, but it was still always cold. Olympic swimmers, including Johnny Weissmuller and Ann Curtis, practiced at Fleishhacker. (Courtesy of a private collector.)

The Southern Pacific Transportation Company donated Locomotive No. 1294 to San Francisco, and in November 1957, the engine was set up in the Fleishhacker Playground near the zoo, as shown at right. Many budding train engineers and railfans spent hours on this engine. (Courtesy of the San Francisco Zoo.)

Here, No. 1294 sits at the zoo in front of a decommissioned cable car, also set in the playground for children's enjoyment. Both the locomotive and the cable car vanished from the playground before 1980. (Courtesy of the San Francisco History Center, San Francisco Public Library.)

This 1929 photograph shows workers clearing and preparing land for the 30-acre Fleishhacker Zoo (now San Francisco Zoo), founded by Herbert Fleishhacker, president of the San Francisco Park Commission. The first residents were from Golden Gate Park—two zebras, one cape buffalo, five rhesus monkeys, and two spider monkeys. Fleishhacker donated three elephants. The zoo now covers 100 acres. (Photograph by T.E. Hect; courtesy of the San Francisco Zoo.)

For 75 years, elephants lived at the zoo, but in the early 2000s, people at the zoo and animal activists disagreed about the elephants' quality of life. In November 2004, the San Francisco Board of Supervisors passed a ban on elephants at the zoo unless a new 15-acre elephant enclosure was built. The last elephant left the zoo in 2004, bound for an animal sanctuary. (Courtesy of the author.)

The theme of elephants at the zoo was strong in 1957, when the elephant train (above) carried thousands of children and adults around the zoo. Every zoo visitor in the 1950s and 1960s seemed to have an elephant key (below). The elephant key was used to activate Talking Storybooks—boxes with stories about exhibits located around the zoo. The keys were also used to describe Storyland exhibits (see the following pages). Many recordings began with a song: "All the animals in the zoo are jumping up and down for you!" (Above, courtesy of the San Francisco History Center, San Francisco Public Library; below, photograph by the author.)

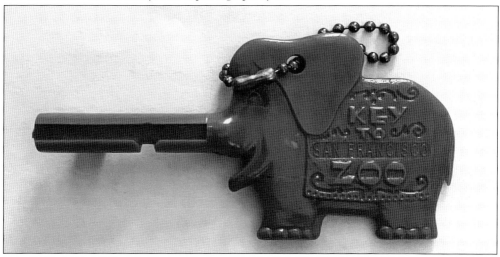

Storyland opened at the San Francisco Zoo in 1959 with scenes inspired by nursery rhymes and fairy tales. The first year of Storyland drew a million visitors. Then attendance declined, and Storyland began to lose money. It slowly disappeared as the site evolved into the Children's Zoo. The final piece of Storyland, Rapunzel's Castle, was torn down in 1996. (Courtesy of the San Francisco History Center, San Francisco Public Library.)

Children entered Storyland through the wondrous Rapunzel's Castle. The main entrance, through the center of the castle, was low. Children could walk right through it and begin exploring the displays, but taller adults had to walk around the castle to enter. (Courtesy of the San Francisco History Center, San Francisco Public Library.)

In Storyland's Old Woman Who Lived in a Shoe exhibit, children climbed steps and rode down a twisting slide. Another scene in Storyland featured the witch's house from Hansel and Gretel. Children entered the door and climbed out through the oven. Jack and Jill were shown tumbling down a hill. Children at the exhibit were like Jack and Jill; they climbed up the hill and rode down on a slide. (Courtesy of the San Francisco History Center, San Francisco Public Library.)

Children and adults looked up at Humpty Dumpty as he seemed to teeter on the edge of a high wall. Some Storyland scenes had audio accompaniment, like Jack Sprat. When people used a zoo elephant key (see page 79), a box near the scene began reciting, "Jack Sprat could eat no fat. His wife could eat no lean." (Courtesy of the San Francisco History Center, San Francisco Public Library.)

81

Amusement rides and concessions appeared at the western edge of San Francisco in the late 19th century. The Whitney brothers, George and Leo, bought the property and opened it in 1926 as Playland-at-the-Beach. At one point, Playland-at-the-Beach featured three blocks of amusements—including a roller coaster, merry-go-round, and fun house—plus various other rides, concessions, and restaurants. Playland-at-the-Beach was popular for more than 50 years. (Courtesy of Ellie Shattuck.)

The Playland-at-the-Beach Funhouse featured a mannequin, Laffing Sal, in the front window. Her recorded manic laugh entertained some children and frightened others. Inside the Funhouse, the features included distorted mirrors, a huge (to a child) rotating tunnel, moving walkways, polished-wood slides, the Joy Wheel (also called the Record Player), and holes in the floor through which sudden air bursts were startling. (Photograph by Dennis O'Rorke.)

The Big Dipper roller coaster (above) was built in 1922. The ride was a hit, although it was never safe; riders were injured and sometimes killed. After the Big Dipper became part of Playland-at-the-Beach in 1936, accidents continued. In 1955, the roller coaster failed a city safety inspection, and it was demolished later that year. The Big Dipper is gone, as is the old streetcar shown here in front of it. (Courtesy of the San Francisco Department of Public Works.)

Playland-at-the-Beach declined in the 1960s. Families started traveling outside San Francisco for recreation and vacations. Some Playland concessions closed, and the park became faded and dirty. A real estate developer purchased Playland-at-the-Beach and closed it over Labor Day weekend in 1972. It was razed immediately, and condominiums were built on the property. (Photograph by Dennis O'Rorke.)

Henry B. Platt built Platt's Music Hall at Montgomery and Bush Streets in 1860. The popular site featured performances by musicians, theatrical groups, mystics, fraternal societies, political parties, and more. It was also the relief headquarters during the floods of 1860 and 1861. Platt's Music Hall was torn down in 1890 and replaced by the Mills Building (offices), which are still standing today. (Courtesy of the San Francisco History Center, San Francisco Public Library.)

In 1898, A.S. Baldwin built Morro Castle, a replica of a Cuban fortress, and Glen Park's Mission Park and Zoological Gardens, hoping to sell real estate lots for a new housing development. Thousands of people came for the festivities, but few bought real estate, and Baldwin sold the grounds in 1901. Soon a new house appeared where Morro Castle had been. (Courtesy of the San Francisco History Center, San Francisco Public Library.)

The Soap Box Derby came to San Francisco in 1936. Not much traffic ran on Sunset Boulevard, especially on weekends. The road was closed on Sundays between Ulloa and Wawona Streets for derby races, which were open only to boys aged 9 to 15. The Bay Area semifinals were held on Sunset Boulevard every summer. (Courtesy of a private collector.)

Built in 1928, Winterland was a venue for opera, boxing, and ice skating. Music promoter Bill Graham began hosting concerts at Winterland in the 1960s. The inset in the top right corner of the image shows concertgoers waiting to get into the building. The last Winterland concert was an all-night performance by the Grateful Dead on New Year's Eve in 1978. The building was torn down in 1985 and replaced by apartments. (Courtesy of a private collector.)

The Bay District Racing Track opened in the Richmond District with harness races in September 1874. The track was soon in decline but then started sponsoring thoroughbred racing. However, the biggest obstacle to the racetrack were Richmond District residents, who criticized it for bringing too much gambling and carousing to their residential neighborhood. The track closed on May 27, 1896. (Courtesy of a private collector.)

J. Cal Ewing built the minor-league park Ewing Field in the Richmond District in 1914. The San Francisco Seals played baseball there for only one season; the ubiquitous summer fog often appeared. The field was leased for circuses and high school and college football games. In 1926, a fire destroyed the bleachers. In 1938, Ewing Terrace, with 95 homes, replaced the ballpark. (Courtesy of a private collector.)

The San Francisco Seals had a long run in Seals Stadium, built at Sixteenth and Bryant Streets in 1931. The Pacific Coast League team played there from 1931 to 1958. When the Giants moved to San Francisco, the team played at Seals Stadium until Candlestick Park was built. Seals Stadium was razed in 1959 and replaced by a shopping center. (Courtesy of the San Francisco History Center, San Francisco Public Library.)

Kezar Stadium was built in the 1920s near the southeast corner of Golden Gate Park for the nearby Polytechnic High School. The stadium eventually attracted professional teams, and the San Francisco 49ers football team played at Kezar from 1946 to 1971. The 1971 film *Dirty Harry* includes a scene filmed at Kezar. It was demolished in 1989 and replaced by a smaller, multiuse stadium called "Little Kezar." (Courtesy of OpenSFHistory, wnp5.50480.)

The San Francisco Giants played baseball at Candlestick Park from 1960 to 1999, but the city's summer weather was too cold for baseball. The 49ers played football there from 1971 to 2013. The last major Beatles concert was held at Candlestick in 1966, and the park is famous for the World Series game that was interrupted by the 1989 Loma Prieta earthquake. Candlestick Park was torn down in 2015. (Courtesy of the Library of Congress.)

The queen of the movie theaters in San Francisco was the magnificent Fox Theatre (right), which opened at 1350 Market Street (near Polk Street) in 1929. Most movie theaters contained 100 to 250 seats, but the Fox had 4,651. It was San Francisco's largest movie theater (250,000 square feet), with the most ornate interior, as shown below. At first, the Fox was popular, selling out plenty of shows, but, like many movie theaters, it began losing audiences with the advent of television in the late 1950s. By the 1960s, the Fox could no longer continue operating. A bond issue to ensure the theater's survival failed. In 1963, the Fox was demolished and replaced by a 29-story business and residence building. (Right, courtesy of the San Francisco Department of Public Works; below, courtesy of OpenSFHistory, wnp5.50514.)

The Coronet Theatre on Geary Boulevard opened on November 2, 1949. Unlike most neighborhood theaters, the Coronet showed first-run movies. In 1955, *Oklahoma!* was at the Coronet—and no other Bay Area theater. People waited in line to watch *Star Wars* in 1977 and again when the trilogy was rereleased in 1997. The theater closed on February 13, 2005, and a senior residence facility replaced it. (Courtesy of OpenSFHistory, wnp5.50480.)

The multiplex Galaxy Theatres opened on February 17, 1984. Some people liked the building's modern lines; others hated them. No marquee advertised the movies, as movie details hung on the back of the building. When business declined in 2002, the Galaxy owners began showing foreign and independent films. The theater closed in 2005 and was demolished six years later. A 14-story apartment building now stands on the site. (Courtesy of Jack Tillmany.)

Six

HOMES AND HOTELS

Unusual events have affected people's lives ever since San Francisco began as Yerba Buena. The multiple fires in the 1850s changed how people built. After each destructive fire, people wanted to rebuild quickly and go back to their lives, hopeful that the next home would not burn down. Life began to settle down after the last major fire in 1851, and people began erecting more permanent residences.

San Franciscans always had a quirky or bohemian side. In the late 19th century, for example, they found a way to use obsolete horsecars and cable cars that had been dumped near the beach. At first, the cars were meeting places for public groups, primarily card-playing and bicycle-riding clubs. Then, people began to make homes out of the abandoned cars, creating a new beach neighborhood called Carville-by-the-Sea. As the neighborhood developed, residents found ways to make the repurposed cars unique, creating multistory homes and other streetcar architecture. After the 1906 earthquake and fires, interest in Carville subsided, as people desired more permanent housing. Carville was soon replaced by traditional houses, schools, and businesses.

San Franciscans continued to look west, and development began on the sand dunes along Lincoln Way just south of Golden Gate Park. Fernando Nelson bought several blocks of sand dunes, and in 1915, he opened a new housing development called Parkway Terrace. Nelson was one of the increasing number of people who were ready to transform sand dunes into thriving neighborhoods.

Fast-forward to the 20th century, when the Del Webb Townehouse motel and Jack Tar Hotel were built. Neither is an example of a great historical hotel, but each had a quirkiness that was part of the San Francisco experience. Both buildings survived for more than 50 years and were recently torn down and replaced—one by new apartments and the other by a medical center.

Life is full of changes, and those changes have frequently occurred around where and how San Franciscans have lived. In the early years, that change came with earthquakes and fires. Now there are various other causes, but the change is still constant.

In the late 19th century, local transportation companies began converting horse-drawn cars to electric cars and cable cars. Some of the obsolete cars were set on undeveloped land near Ocean Beach and offered for sale for $10 each, or $20 with seats. The cars first became popular as meeting places for bicycle clubs and card-playing groups. Eventually, people began using them as homes. (Courtesy of OpenSFHistory, Marilyn Blaisdell Collection, wnp70.0815.)

People in what was called Carville-by-the-Sea (sometimes "Car Town") sometimes put two cars together to create an L-shaped home, as shown here. Another creation had three cars put together in a U shape to make a private courtyard protected from the wind and sand. (Courtesy of Marilyn Blaisdell.)

Some people in Carville stacked cars to make two- and three-story homes, as shown in this 1905 photograph. One multistory Carville house (not shown) opened as a hotel and later became a church. After 1906, people were looking for more permanent homes, and Carville disappeared as the area was developed. (Photograph by Randolph Brandt; courtesy of Emiliano Echeverria.)

Another obsolete cable-car community was established after the 1906 earthquake by Dr. Charles V. Cross in the Inner Richmond District. Cross created the Carzonia Apartments on his property along the block between California and Cornwall Streets near Fifth Avenue. His own home at 2808 California Street was one of these apartments. Carzonia did not last long; a traditional building was erected in 1911. (Courtesy of a private collector.)

At one time, cozy cottages like this one at 420 Thirty-Third Avenue were scattered around the Richmond District. Some of these cottages remain in the Richmond; others have been torn down to make space for larger developments. This house and the one next to it no longer exist. Most of the block is now covered with two- to three-story apartment houses. (Courtesy of John Freeman.)

These three Victorians once stood at 2213–2217 Van Ness Avenue. It is not clear whether they burned during the 1906 fire (which stopped at Van Ness Avenue) or if they were later razed and then replaced by the modern buildings that stand here now. The two partially visible buildings on the left and right are still extant. (Courtesy of the Library of Congress.)

Sand dunes were common in San Francisco until the 20th century. This c. 1900 photograph looks west toward the Pacific Ocean. Sand dunes and associated plants are all that is visible. The object near the water at right is one of the two Golden Gate Park windmills. Today, everything except the ocean, beach, and windmill has been completely covered by development. (Courtesy of a private collector.)

In 1915, builder Fernando Nelson began planning Parkway Terrace, a housing development in the Sunset District. He started by constructing concrete ornamental benches on Lincoln Way at the corners of Twenty-Seventh through Thirty-Third Avenues. This 1918 photograph shows a completed bench in front of sand dunes—within 10 years, this view of the dunes would disappear forever as houses and streets were built. (Courtesy of Emiliano Echeverria.)

The Jack Tar Hotel opened on Van Ness Avenue in 1960 and was advertised as "the world's most modern hotel," with a rooftop ice-skating rink and electronic check-in. San Franciscans always had a love-hate relationship with the building. The hotel's name was changed to Cathedral Hill in 1982, and it closed on October 30, 2009. It was razed four years later and replaced by the California Pacific Medical Center. (Courtesy of the Library of Congress.)

In 1959, Delbert "Del" Webb bought the Crystal Palace Market (page 66) and replaced it with the Del Webb Townehouse, a 400-room luxury motel that cost $8 million to build. The Townehouse was part of a 1972 episode of *The Streets of San Francisco*. The motel was not a success. In 2013, it was torn down and replaced by Trinity Place, a group of modern buildings with 1,900 luxury apartments. (Courtesy of John Freeman.)

In early February 1992, the large apartment building on the cliff above the Filbert Street steps began to move, and residents were evacuated. People started gathering at the bottom to "encourage" the house to fall; soon, the gawkers were cheering for the building to withstand engineers' efforts. On Sunday, February 29, workers pulled the building away from the cliff. It fell and was destroyed when it hit the ground below. (Courtesy of the Library of Congress.)

In December 1995, after extensive rain, a century-old storm and sewage line collapsed in the Seacliff area. The escaping water created an 8,000-square-foot sinkhole. Before long, an 80-year-old, three-story mansion fell into the sinkhole and was destroyed. The light-colored house near the left side of this photograph was undermined and thought to be doomed, but city engineers saved it; it still stands today. The mansion was never rebuilt. (Courtesy of the author.)

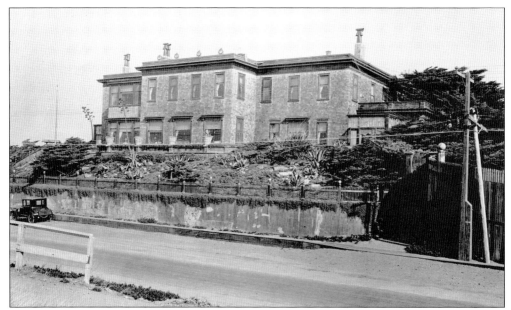

This house was built in the 1850s on the Great Highway. Over the next 90 years, it was a roadhouse (Oceanside House); a home for Alexander and Ida Russell, who are credited with introducing Zen philosophies to America; and Tait's at the Beach, which provided food and music for a decade. Tait's closed in 1931, and the building was destroyed by fire in 1940. (Courtesy of a private collector.)

In 1885, city benefactor and property owner Adolph Sutro had his house built on 20 acres at the end of Point Lobos Avenue, overlooking the Cliff House. He surrounded his house with gardens and statuary. This photograph shows Sutro next to his house. The land was later donated to San Francisco and became Sutro Heights Park. The house, statuary, and gardens no longer exist. (Courtesy of the Library of Congress.)

Seven

MISCELLANEOUS

This chapter contains many things that do not belong in a specific category but have also vanished. Some buildings in this chapter have unique features. For example, the Parrott Block, built of granite blocks made in China, survived the 1906 earthquake and fire. Another building that survived the 1906 disaster was the Montgomery Block, built in 1853. The What Cheer House was one of the thousands of buildings destroyed in 1906, but it was unique in that it contained the first library and museum in San Francisco. Unfortunately, it was open only to white men, which was a frequent restriction at that time.

At least 10 mile houses were built in and south of San Francisco. These businesses offered places to stay, food and drink, and water for horses. The Six Mile House in San Francisco was demolished in 1938 for a garage and gas station, and now only one mile house remains.

Some places reflect San Francisco's growth. By the 20th century, the city's population had grown so much that the five cemeteries in the Richmond District were moved out of the city so housing could be built. The Hall of Justice on Kearny Street was torn down to be replaced by a Holiday Inn (now a Hilton Hotel). The 75-year-old Engine 15 Firehouse was demolished to make way for a larger modern firehouse.

Of course, some items make people nostalgic. The ubiquitous gasholders are frequently remembered with sentimental attachments. They seemed to be everywhere, in all neighborhoods. No one seemed to notice their disappearance, but now, when people see photographs, they become nostalgic. The response is similar for the two-toned foghorns (or any foghorns), as well as the Hamm's and Coca-Cola signs. The Irving Street gas station had a dramatic pull for people who wanted to see this long-closed brick structure preserved and used in some new way. However, its corner lot made it very attractive to developers.

Many other items fit in this chapter's "miscellaneous" category.

R.B. Woodward, founder of Woodward's Gardens (see page 72), opened the What Cheer House (left) in 1852. It was a unique hotel at 527–529 Sacramento Street at Leidesdorff Street. What Cheer was open to men only, allowed no liquor on the premises, and housed San Francisco's first free library and first museum. Its library featured bookplates (below) that gave the rules of the library and reading room, including no talking, sleeping, or smoking, and noted that no books should be taken from the library. The What Cheer Restaurant opened next door, at 525 Sacramento Street, by 1868. The hotel also had its own laundry. The What Cheer House was destroyed by the 1906 earthquake and fire. (Left, courtesy of the San Francisco History Center, San Francisco Public Library; below, courtesy of the Sutro Library Branch, California State Library.)

NOTICE.

WHAT CHEER HOUSE
LIBRARY & READING ROOM.

Gentlemen will please replace books in their proper number after using them.

No Talking, Sleeping or Smoking allowed in this room.

Books Newspapers and Periodicals must not be destroyed, NOR TAKEN FROM THIS ROOM.

$10 REWARD

will be paid for information that will convict any person of stealing books from this house.

Open from 6 a.m., till 10 p.m.

R. B. WOODWARD,
PROPRIETOR.

San Francisco's first city hall was located at 700 Kearny Street between Clay and Washington Streets. The building opened in 1851 as the third Jenny Lind Theatre. (The first two theaters had burned down in fires earlier that year.) In 1852, the city bought the building and used it as city hall until the new city hall opened in Civic Center in 1897. A high-rise Hilton Hotel now stands in this location. (Courtesy of the Library of Congress.)

San Francisco's first French Hospital opened in 1851 on Rincon Hill and moved to Bryant Street in 1856. In 1895, this French Hospital was built on Point Lobos (now Geary Boulevard) near Sixth Avenue. The location was chosen because of the fresh breezes on Point Lobos. In 1963, it was razed and replaced by a modern French Hospital. The French Campus has been part of Kaiser Permanente since 1989. (Courtesy of John Freeman.)

The Engine 15 Firehouse, located at 2150 California Street, was built in what might be derisively called Gothic Burlesque, a style that was popular in San Francisco from the 1850s through the 1880s. Built in 1884, the firehouse was one of the principal buildings of this style to survive the 1906 earthquake and fire. It was demolished in 1959 and replaced by a modern firehouse. (Courtesy of the Library of Congress.)

The San Francisco Hall of Justice and County Jail was built at 50 Kearny Street in 1910. It was demolished in December 1967 and replaced by a Holiday Inn. The old hall of justice is best remembered from a television show—exterior film of the building showed it serving as the police headquarters on television's *Ironside* series, which ran from 1967 to 1975. (Courtesy of the Library of Congress.)

Hall of Justice, San Francisco, California.

In the 1930s, the University of California, San Francisco (UCSF), hired muralist Bernard Zakheim (with assistant Phyllis Wrightson) to paint a set of murals telling the history of medicine in California. The above panel focuses on medical incidents in San Francisco history. For years, the Zakheim murals provided the backdrop for medical classes in UCSF's Toland Hall. However, some faculty members found the murals distracting. They were painted over, and framed portraits of faculty members were posted on the walls. Later, the murals were uncovered and restored. In 2021, the mural panels were taken down and put in storage; they have again vanished from view and are no longer available for people to see. (Above, photograph by Chris Carlsson; right, courtesy of University of California, San Francisco.)

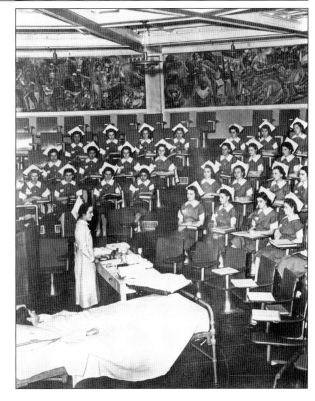

This 1915 Chevalier map of San Francisco shows the cemeteries that once operated in the eastern part of the Richmond District. It looks as if all the residential streets were already in place, but the first map of the Richmond was drawn in 1860 with the future streets and lots in place. By 1945, all of these cemeteries had been closed, and the land was prepared for housing development.

The first Richmond cemetery opened in 1854. Lone Mountain Cemetery was named after a popular hill (shown here) about one and a half miles south. It was renamed Laurel Hill Cemetery in 1867. According to a plaque that was once on a nearby wall, Laurel Hill was known as the resting place for "the builders of the West, civic and military leaders, jurists, inventors, artists, and eleven United States Senators." The cemetery shown here is Odd Fellows, which is described on the following page. (Courtesy of a private collector.)

This 1940 photograph shows the deteriorating Laurel Hill Cemetery with the growing city in the background. The cemetery closed in the late 1930s. In 1939 and 1940, remains were moved to Cypress Lawn Cemetery in Colma, California. (Courtesy of the San Francisco History Center, San Francisco Public Library.)

The Odd Fellows Cemetery opened in 1864 for members of the Odd Fellows fraternal organization. The families of the dead had to pay for remains to be reburied in Colma. However, in the case of the Odd Fellows Cemetery, the people collecting the money disappeared, so all the remains are buried under one marker in Colma. (Courtesy of a private collector.)

The Masonic Cemetery opened in 1864. In this undated photograph, part of the cemetery is at the front left of the image. Housing has been built right up to the cemetery's border. San Francisco was eager to remove the cemeteries so more housing could be built. In the 1930s, approximately 20,000 remains were moved from the Masonic Cemetery to Woodlawn Cemetery in Colma. (Courtesy of the San Francisco History Center, San Francisco Public Library.)

The Point Lobos Toll Road opened in 1863, running from what is now Geary Boulevard and Presidio Avenue to the beach. This photograph shows the road next to Calvary Cemetery, which opened in 1860 for Roman Catholics. Between 1939 and 1941, approximately 50,000 remains were moved from Calvary Cemetery to Holy Cross Cemetery in Colma. (Courtesy of a private collector.)

Businesses that commonly open near cemeteries include stonemasons, florists, and pubs. Around 1899, Carl Zulk opened C.J. Zulk Monumental Works (above) close to the Odd Fellows Cemetery at what is now the corner of Geary Boulevard and Stanyan Street. Shortly after this business opened, the San Francisco Board of Supervisors expressed an eagerness to close the cemeteries and replace them with housing; in 1901, the board required that all San Francisco cemeteries be closed to new burials. It took another 30 years to empty the cemeteries, move the remains to Colma, and prepare the land for development. In the below photograph, which was taken on December 26, 1933, men are removing remains so the Odd Fellows Cemetery could be developed into housing and Rossi Park. (Above, courtesy of John Freeman; below, courtesy of a private collector.)

The Xerces blue butterfly (*Glaucopsyche xerces*) was the first North American butterfly known to become extinct because of human activity. The Xerces was native to sand dunes and common in San Francisco's Sunset District. Development in the Sunset during the 1930s and 1940s destroyed the lupine and other native dune plants essential to the growth of this butterfly. The species was declared extinct in the early 1940s. (Courtesy of Xerces.org.)

George Washington High School stands in San Francisco's Richmond District. Before the site contained a school, it housed a rock quarry. Various quarries operated around San Francisco, drawing out rock for bricks, cobblestones, street paving, construction, bay fill, and other uses. George Washington High School opened in 1936, and today, there is no sign of the quarry. (Courtesy of a private collector.)

Built in 1853, the Montgomery Block (also known as the Monkey Block) was a four-story building at 628 Montgomery Street. The Montgomery Block was designed to be earthquake-resistant and fireproof; it lived up to this reputation in 1906, when it was one of the major buildings in the Financial District to survive the earthquake and fire. When the block was first built, it was the headquarters of professional men and businesses. During the 1930s and the Depression, writers and artists—including Jack London, Emma Goldman, and George Sterling—began living there, and it became a bohemian center. At one time, 75 painters, sculptors, writers, photographers, and musicians had studios there. It was demolished in 1959. Today, another impressive and easily recognized building stands in its place: the Transamerica Pyramid (right). (Above, photograph by A.J. Wittlock, courtesy of the Library of Congress; right, photograph by Ron Henggeler.)

During the California Gold Rush, laundry service was so expensive that many men sent their clothes to China or Hawaii for cleaning. Women began earning money by washing laundry in a pristine lake bounded by today's Lombard, Filbert, Gough, and Octavia Streets. The lake became known as Washerwoman's Lagoon (at left in the above image). Over time, the water became polluted by the washing, the neighborhoods growing nearby, and the area's slaughterhouses, tanneries, and factories. In 1877, the lake was filled in. The below photograph shows that today, there is no sign of Washerwoman's Lagoon. (Above, courtesy of the San Francisco History Center, San Francisco Public Library; below, courtesy of the National Park Service.)

In 1852, banker and importer John Parrott hired Chinese laborers to erect the three-story Parrott Block at California and Montgomery Streets using granite blocks imported from China. Unlike most downtown buildings, the Parrott Block (at far left in this image from the late 1800s) was not damaged by the 1906 earthquake. When it was torn down in 1926, newspapers speculated that Mexican doubloons, gold, and jewels were in the debris. (Courtesy of the Library of Congress.)

In 1882, the Casino restaurant and bar was built just west of the Conservatory of Flowers in Golden Gate Park. Because it served liquor, park commissioners feared it was out of character with the park's "wholesome" image, so the Casino was moved outside the park in 1896. The Casino was torn down in 1922, when housing began to fill the neighborhood. (Courtesy of the San Francisco History Center, San Francisco Public Library.)

432. North Beach and Meiggs' Wharf, from Russian Hill, San Francisco.

Harry Meiggs came to San Francisco in 1849. In 1853, he built Meiggs' Wharf, a huge L-shaped lumber pier jutting out from the base of Mason Street more than 1,600 feet into the bay. As the city began filling in the bay, the shops and warehouses on Meiggs' Wharf disappeared. The pier burned on the second day of the fire following the 1906 earthquake. (Courtesy of the Library of Congress.)

Many ships sank off the coast of San Francisco because of the rough, rocky waters and foggy weather. The SS *Ohioan* was built in 1914; on October 8, 1936, the *Ohioan* ran aground near Seal Rocks. Five months later, a fire started on the ship, and it broke into two pieces. For years afterward, people could still see the *Ohioan*'s wreckage. (Courtesy of Rita Dunn.)

People often wonder where the beach is in the neighborhood named North Beach. This 1866 photograph shows the beach that was originally there. At one time, North Beach was on the north coast of San Francisco. As in many coastal areas in San Francisco, part of the bay was filled in during the 19th century; in this case, the fill eliminated the beach. (Courtesy of the Library of Congress.)

The Mission Bay neighborhood was once a bay on the east shore of San Francisco. It was a natural habitat for ducks, geese, herons, and ospreys. It became a dumping ground for building projects in the mid-1800s and later for debris from the 1906 earthquake. Mission Bay was filled in, and after becoming a city redevelopment project in 1998, it evolved into a wealthy neighborhood. (Courtesy of Peter Linenthal.)

Mount Olympus stands at the geographical center of San Francisco. It once provided unobstructed views of the Farallon Islands and Point Reyes, as well as the city's hills and Golden Gate Park. In 1887, city benefactor Adolph Sutro saw the *Triumph of Light* sculpture by Belgian artist Antoine Wiertz (1806–1865) and ordered a replica of it. Sutro donated the replica on a pedestal to San Francisco at Mount Olympus. (Photograph by I.W. Taber; courtesy of OpenSFHistory, wnp27.6960.)

At the 1887 unveiling of *Triumph of Light*, Adolph Sutro proclaimed, "May the light shine from the goddess of Liberty to inspire our citizens to good and noble deeds for the benefit of mankind." Photographs from 1927 (above) and 1947 (below) show that while buildings were constructed around Mount Olympus, for a long time, the view remained wide open, and the statue still stood tall. However, the area changed considerably in the ensuing years. (Above, courtesy of the San Francisco Department of Public Works; below, courtesy of the San Francisco History Center, San Francisco Public Library.)

For many years, *Triumph of Light* was the victim of municipal neglect and destructive vandalism. The statue was finally removed in the 1950s. The San Francisco Recreation and Parks Department maintains the gardens beautifully, but all that remains of *Triumph of Light* are the pedestal, which is almost 20 feet tall, and the stairs leading to it, which are surrounded by tall trees, parked cars, and buildings. Most of the views are now gone. (Photograph by the author.)

The University of California, San Francisco, opened as a hospital on Parnassus Avenue in 1907. This 1909 image below shows two of the original buildings at the university medical center, as well as a rare sightseeing streetcar. All of the buildings have been replaced, and streetcars no longer operate on Parnassus Avenue. (Courtesy of Emiliano Echeverria.)

The brick building shown above, located on Irving Street at Sixteenth Avenue, was a Mohawk gas station that opened in 1926. At one point, the owner planned to supplement his meager income by selling cars. He bought the lot facing the gas station to open a Pontiac car showroom, but the San Francisco Fire Department took the land using eminent domain and built Fire House 22. The gas station stayed in business and continued to provide car servicing, but it finally closed in the 1950s. The service bay was demolished in 2012, but the brick building remained. It had many supporters who hoped to find a way to preserve it as a café or other community building. However, one day in 2018, the little brick structure was quickly torn down (below). (Above, courtesy of a private collector; below, photograph by Bruce Eng.)

The original Parkside Elementary School (above) was a small one-room building located on Taraval Street near Thirty-First Avenue. After the school closed in 1917, the St. Cecilia Catholic parish was forming and wanted to build a church. James "Sunny Jim" Rolph was the mayor of San Francisco at the time, and he decided to do something a politician would never do today—donate the one-room schoolhouse to the Catholic archdiocese to use in building its new church (below) at Fifteenth Avenue and Taraval Street. In 1957, the parish was able to build a much larger church at 2555 Seventeenth Avenue, and the old school turned church was no longer needed. (Both, courtesy of the Archdiocese of San Francisco.)

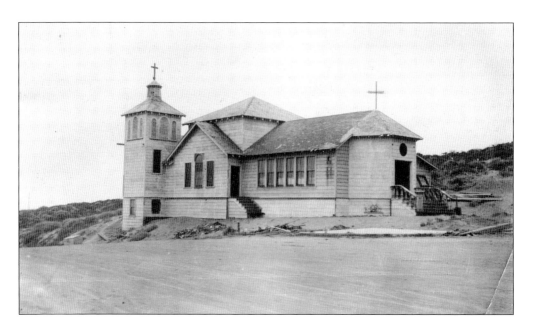

In 1922, the San Francisco Public School District built a new Parkside School (above) on Twenty-Fifth Avenue between Ulloa and Vicente Streets. It served children from kindergarten through sixth grade and included a large auditorium and two large play yards, one for kindergarten through third graders and girls and the other for boys above third grade. The below photograph, taken in the "girls' schoolyard," shows that the buildings surrounded the yards on the north and west sides. Parkside School closed in 1975, and the buildings were used by the school district for a few years. Neighborhood residents were torn between wanting to restore the school or tear it down and build a new one. Parkside was razed in 2004 and replaced by Dianne Feinstein Elementary School. (Above, courtesy of the San Francisco History Center, San Francisco Public Library; below, photograph by the author.)

Gasholders, or gasometers, appeared around San Francisco from the early 1900s through the 1960s. These enormous metal containers stored up to two million cubic feet of natural gas. The movable cap rose and fell depending on how much gas was being stored. The above postcard shows a gasholder in Fisherman's Wharf; the below photograph shows one near Islais Creek. Gasholders began to disappear from San Francisco when the technology of gas storage changed. (Above, courtesy of John Freeman; below, courtesy of the San Francisco Department of Public Works.)

Dogpatch used to be more industrial than most city areas, but it still had a gasholder (above). By the 1980s, energy infrastructure had started to improve, and the use of gasholders steadily declined. The below photograph of an empty gasholder was taken in 1980, when the structures were disappearing. Today, gasholders do not exist in San Francisco. (Above, courtesy of the author; below, photograph by Susan Saperstein.)

The City of Paris, a popular clothing store, opened downtown in 1850 and moved to Stockton and Geary Streets in 1896. The structure was damaged by fire in 1906 and rebuilt. The store permanently closed on March 25, 1972. People fought to save the building from destruction, but it was razed in 1980. (Courtesy of the Library of Congress.)

Soon after the City of Paris closed, the site was sold. After years of delay, destruction began in 1980, and Neiman Marcus opened in 1981. Although the City of Paris was gone, the stained-glass rotunda from that popular store survived and was placed above the Neiman Marcus tearoom. (Photograph by Carol M. Highsmith; courtesy of the Library of Congress.)

Mile houses were places where, from 1849 to the early 1900s, stagecoach riders could give water to their horses and lodging and strong drink to themselves. Each house was named for the number of miles it stood from a major city building. The Six Mile House, shown here, was on Bayshore Boulevard near Visitacion Avenue; it was demolished in 1938. Today, only the Seven Mile House remains standing. (Courtesy of the Library of Congress.)

In 1976, John Wehrle and John Rampley painted *Positively Fourth Street*, which was located on an outside wall at Golden Gate Park's de Young Museum. It showed the Fourth Street exit off Freeway 80 in an abandoned San Francisco. Buildings and the road are crumbling, and animals explore the roadway. The painting, which remained outdoors for several years, deteriorated and was moved to Fort Mason, where it further deteriorated and was finally removed. (Photograph by James Petrillo; courtesy of John Rampley.)

From 1938 to 2021, a bright red sign promoting Coca-Cola stood in this spot south of Market Street. It would be dark, then suddenly light up, sparkle a bit, and go dark again. Originally neon, it was later changed to use LED lights. Some people were sorry to see it go; others felt it was just an advertisement. Few signs have lasted that long in San Francisco. (Courtesy of the Library of Congress.)

To the delight of Central Freeway riders, a neon sign was installed in 1954 on top of the Hamm's Beer brewery at 1550 Bryant Street. It showed a 13-foot-high glass filling with beer, complete with a white foam head at the top. The brewery closed in 1975, and the glass disappeared. The building now contains offices; the sign is long gone. (Photograph by Bob Campbell; courtesy of the San Francisco Chronicle.)

To aid vessels as they pass under the Golden Gate Bridge, foghorns have been mounted on the bridge since it opened in 1937. Today, three foghorns are mounted below the roadway level at mid-span and two are on the south-tower pier. Depending on the visibility under the bridge, workers manually turn the foghorns on and off. The original foghorns were two-toned, and many San Franciscans are nostalgic about them. In the late 1970s, one of the original 1937 foghorns stopped working when its two air valves gave out, and the two-tone horn became one-toned. The mechanism was old, and replacement parts were not available, so in 1985, the horns were replaced with new single-tone horns. People can still hear single-toned foghorns in San Francisco, but they can no longer hear the old two-toned foghorns. (Photograph by Robert K. Bryant.)

INDEX

DISCOVER THOUSANDS OF LOCAL HISTORY BOOKS
FEATURING MILLIONS OF VINTAGE IMAGES

Arcadia Publishing, the leading local history publisher in the United States, is committed to making history accessible and meaningful through publishing books that celebrate and preserve the heritage of America's people and places.

Find more books like this at
www.arcadiapublishing.com

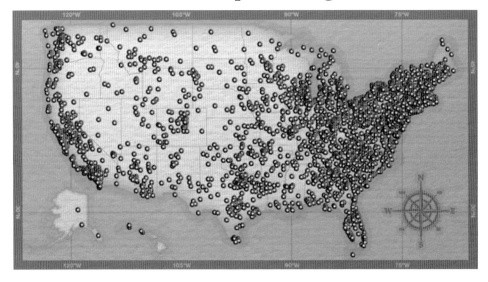

Search for your hometown history, your old stomping grounds, and even your favorite sports team.

Consistent with our mission to preserve history on a local level, this book was printed in South Carolina on American-made paper and manufactured entirely in the United States. Products carrying the accredited Forest Stewardship Council (FSC) label are printed on 100 percent FSC-certified paper.

MADE IN THE USA